THE

Curious Nature

GUIDE

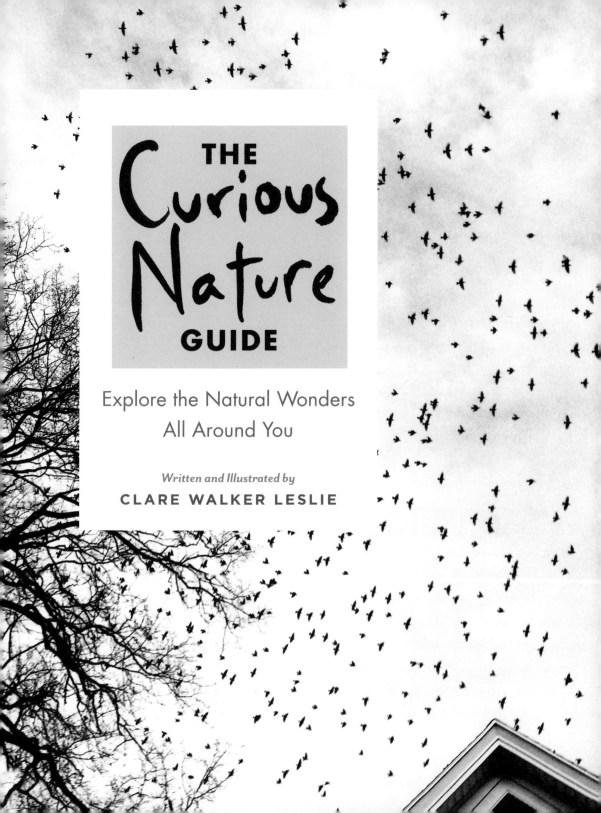

THE
Curious
Nature
GUIDE

Explore the Natural Wonders
All Around You

Written and Illustrated by
CLARE WALKER LESLIE

The mission of Storey Publishing is to serve our customers by
publishing practical information that encourages
personal independence in harmony with the environment.

Edited by DEBORAH BALMUTH and
HANNAH FRIES

Additional editorial assistance by
REBECCA BACKMAN

Art direction and book design by
CAROLYN ECKERT

Illustrations by © CLARE WALKER LESLIE

Cover photography by Carolyn Eckert, back
(middle right & bottom), back flap (top), front flap
(bottom left); © Dean Casavechia, back (middle
left); © Evan Sheppard, front flap (top); © Heather
Perry, back (top), back flap (middle), front flap
(bottom right); © Jamie Goldenberg, back flap
(bottom); © Mark Fleming, front flap (middle);
© Michelle Albert/Getty Images, front (leaves);
© Peter Haigh/Getty Images, front (background)

Interior photography credits appear on page 143

Map on page 93 by Ilona Sherratt

© 2015 by Clare Walker Leslie

The information in this book is true and complete
to the best of our knowledge. All recommenda-
tions are made without guarantee on the part
of the author or Storey Publishing. The author
and publisher disclaim any liability in connection
with the use of this information.

Storey books are available for special premium
and promotional uses and for customized
editions. For further information, please call
1-800-793-9396.

Storey Publishing
210 MASS MoCA Way
North Adams, MA 01247
www.storey.com

Printed in China by Toppan Leefung Printing Ltd.
10 9 8 7 6 5 4 3 2

Library of Congress Cataloging-in-Publication
Data on file

Contents

Introduction

How does nature fit into your life?

Whether or not you have a garden or time to go to the Galapagos, you have opened this book, so perhaps you are curious about the strange and wild world of nature that is all around you.

starling

pigeon

crow

hawk

duck

robin

Do you have these birds near you?

Maybe you feel the need to reconnect.

Maybe you have noticed you feel better after some time outdoors. Maybe you find you're getting a bit curious about the trees or birds, plants or insects in your neighborhood.

If nature has generally been something you have been afraid of, don't worry: the best antidote to the unknown is to learn as much as you can. Learning about nature takes you wherever you are and leads you wherever you want to go — to the seashore, on a hike, to a backyard garden, to a birding group, to a biology class, to a library. It's something you can do alone, with a friend, or with a group of people.

Consider this book a companion.
Leave it by your window to remind
you to look outside. Take it to
work for when you need a break.
Put it by your bed to inspire dreams
and plans. Bring it with you when
you travel.

Exploring nature knows no age limit,
no skill requirement, no time limit,
no location or destination. It is a
longstanding tradition that spans
countries and centuries. Many
people find that in learning about
the natural world, they learn more
about themselves.

Let's begin the adventure.

BEGIN

Begin Where You Are

No matter where you are right now, look up and out any window. Or go stand in a doorway. Or step outside. Is it day or night, sunny or cloudy, cool or warm? Count to five and just watch, silently, what the world of nature is doing around you. Forget for a moment where you need to be and where you have come from.

TRY THIS
List six or seven nature observations you see, hear, or feel. Also consider items made from nature. Note the time of day, month, date, and season, as well as your location.

EXAMPLE:
blue sky, bare tree branches, sparrows on wire, wind blowing, squirrel looking for what?, asphalt, yellow leaves on the ground

10:40 a.m., October 10, early fall, Cambridge, MA, from our apartment window

clouds moving in from South →

Waxing moon setting in West

evening planet

2 pigeons getting last sunset warmth

Norway maple and basswood

purp purp

Along our street at dusk
September 18   6:40 pm   68°
tree crickets, 1 robin, 1 blue jay
dog barking   smells of drying leaves

13

Sitting at a stoplight, a red-tailed hawk watching the traffic below

Take a One-Minute Vacation

There are 1,440 minutes in each day, which we quickly fill. Before you leap in the car, hop on a bus, walk the dog, or head to work, pause for a minute and stand still. Look around and just notice — the sky, tree shapes, birds, any plants or insects. Take a snapshot with your eyes. Breathe deeply; hear your heart. Close your eyes and listen. Feel the sun or wind or cold on your face.

Use just 3 of those 1,440 minutes to connect with the nature around you, and then move on with your day. In some meditation practices this is called, simply, "being in the present moment." It costs nothing, can be done anywhere at any time, and no one else needs to know you are pausing.

How do you feel after pausing? What are you thinking about?

multiflora rosehips

sugar maple leaf

raspberries

rosa rugosa hips

TRY THIS
Give yourself an assignment the next time you go outside:

Look for things in nature that are somehow alike.

You can alter your assignment by changing the rules — for example, find things in nature that are red, or round, or that have interesting textures or smells. If you want, collect small objects to bring home for an arrangement, or just take a photo of them.

Learning to See in a Different Way

It takes time to slow down, untangle our busy minds and daily schedules, and just stop and notice the world around us, the little things as well as the big things. Nature's patterns are ours, too — day, night, cold, warm, rain, sun, winter to summer and back again.

If I had influence with the good fairy . . . I should ask that her gift to each child in the world be a sense of wonder so indestructible that it would last throughout life. — RACHEL CARSON, *THE SENSE OF WONDER*

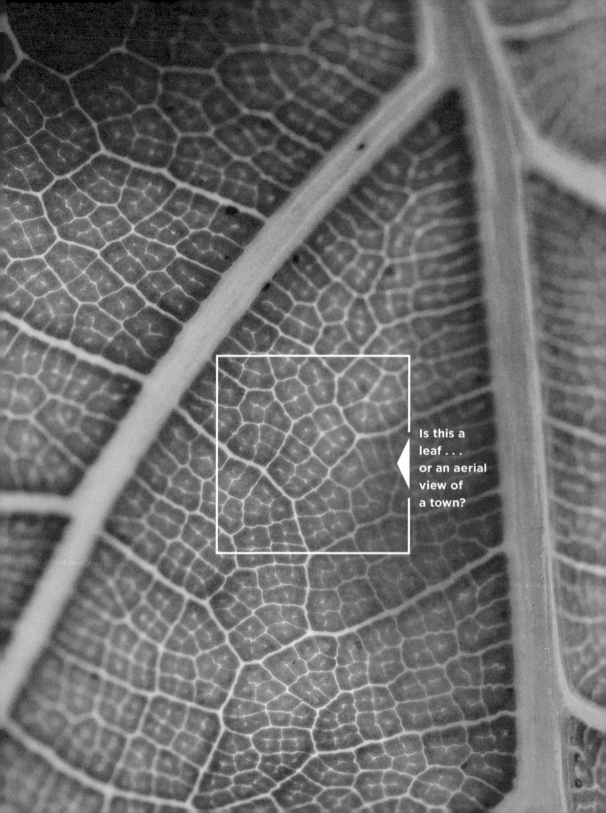

Is this a leaf . . . or an aerial view of a town?

Follow Your Ears, Nose, and Fingertips

As you walk, bike, run, or simply sit
on your porch, try to notice the natural
things around you. Imagine that you
are blind (perhaps you can have someone
blindfold you and lead you around).

Put your nose deep into a flower.

Listen for bird chatter or insects.

Feel the coolness of a rock.

Explore the texture of bark.

We humans tend to use our eyes more than other senses when we are observing. Favor another sense for a while.

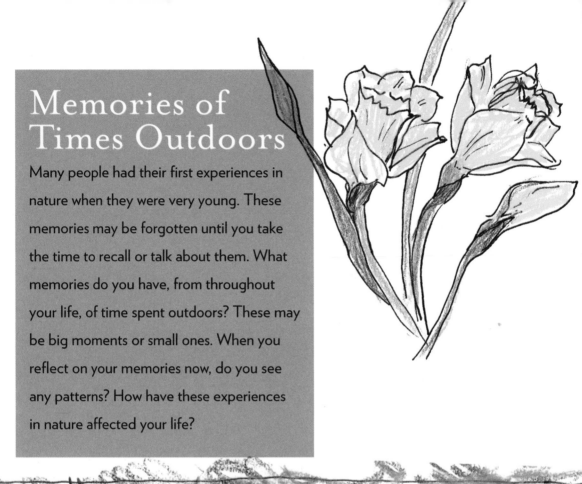

Memories of Times Outdoors

Many people had their first experiences in nature when they were very young. These memories may be forgotten until you take the time to recall or talk about them. What memories do you have, from throughout your life, of time spent outdoors? These may be big moments or small ones. When you reflect on your memories now, do you see any patterns? How have these experiences in nature affected your life?

Think about
four memorable
outdoor
experiences.

TRY THIS
Have you ever . . . ?

- **climbed a tree**
- **caught a frog**
- **jumped off rocks**
- **followed a river path**
- **gone apple picking**
- **chased fireflies**

backyard bunnies

Memories are often linked to smells.

A woman told me that in remembering her home in India, she realized that it is the smell of the mud and moisture in the air before it rains that she misses the most. Are there certain smells that trigger memories for you? Rain on hot pavement, fresh-cut grass, pine needles . . . ?

Sounds can be linked to memories too. For me, the pulsing calls of the snowy tree crickets outside my window on hot September nights in Pennsylvania mix with memories of having to go back to school. What sounds evoke memories for you?

snowy tree cricket

Did You Know?

Our skin cells have more than 15 of the olfactory receptors found in the nose. Amazingly, olfactory receptors — which detect specific chemicals — have been found in several other organs, including the liver, heart, lungs, colon, and brain. Genetic evidence suggests that nearly every organ in the body contains olfactory receptors.

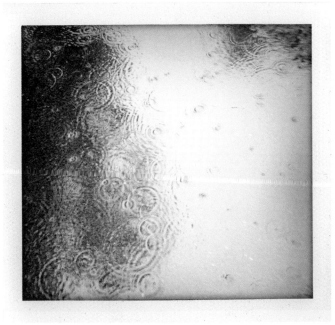

Plum Island
Winter light
on ice
1:30 pm
1.18.02

Time for a Ramble

Find some time to roam outdoors. Make a date with nature
and put it on your calendar, as you would any appointment.
It could be for 15 minutes, 30 minutes, 2 hours, or as long
as you want. Daydream about it, or when you lie down to
go to sleep, ponder where you might go.

Not that a ramble afield makes everything okay, just like that. But going out, alert and open, causes some chamber of the heart that has temporarily drained to pump again. You can remember that you can harbor loss, hold tight to sorrow, and honor grief, while still rejoicing in the rich gifts of the Earth. . . . In a world deeply flawed . . . this is no small potatoes.

— ROBERT M. PYLE

ORION, MARCH/APRIL 2005

TRY THIS

What nearby plants and animals do you already know?

Start a list and add to it as the seasons change and you get better at noticing.

Put a date and location beside each entry. Why not tack your list on the refrigerator or on a wall so family, friends, or co-workers can add to it too?

Once you begin noticing, you will see more and more.

Your Home Place

How would you describe the natural
landscape where you live? Is it hilly,
flat, wooded, arid, mountainous, agricultural,
coastal, forested, urban, suburban, rural?

What makes your home place distinct from other places?

Has it changed since you've lived there?

But maybe it's for just that reason — how busy we are and distracted and disconnected we are — that wonder really is a survival skill. It might be the thing that reminds us of what really matters, and of the greater systems that our lives are completely dependent on. It might be the thing that helps us build an emotional connection — an intimacy — with our surroundings that, in turn, would make us want to do anything we can to protect them.

— H. EMERSON BLAKE,
IN THE FOREWORD TO
*WONDER AND OTHER
SURVIVAL SKILLS*

Tuscon AZ 4·19 7:39 pm

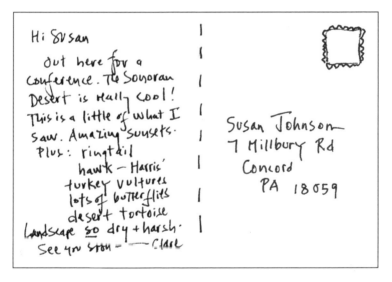

Hi Susan

Out here for a conference. The Sonoran Desert is really cool! This is a little of what I saw. Amazing sunsets. Plus: ringtail hawk — Harris' turkey vultures lots of butterflies desert tortoise Landscape _so_ dry + harsh. See you soon — Clare

Susan Johnson
7 Millbury Rd
Concord
PA 18059

Making Maps

Making a map of where you live or where you've traveled can help you see
your relationship to the bigger picture — your neighborhood, your town or city,
your state or province, your country, the world.

TRY THIS
Make a map of your neighborhood, walking route, or a remembered place from childhood.

**Keep it simple. No need to worry about scale or accuracy. It's your map, so
be creative! When you travel, it can be useful to draw a map to help you remember
either where you are going or where you have been. This can be especially
fun if you combine it with photos or a journal.**

Small glimpses:

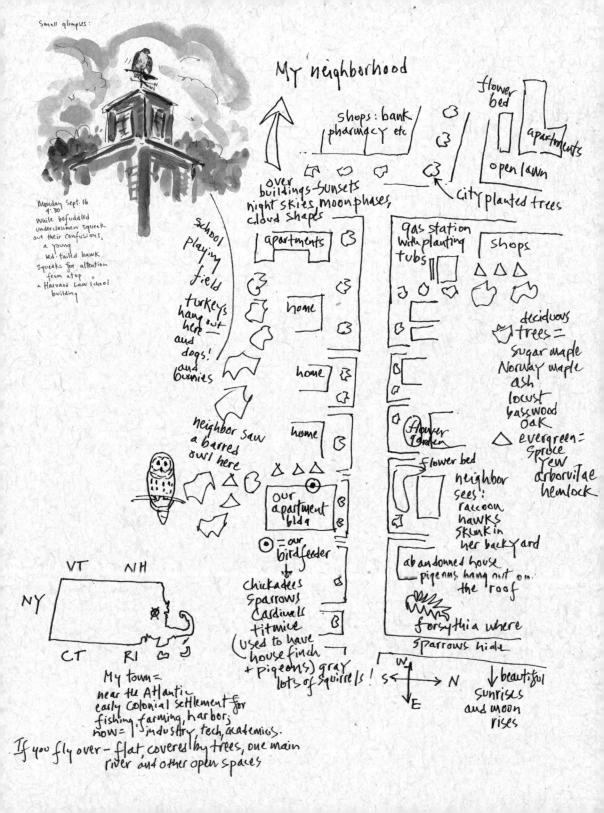

Monday Sept. 16
4:30
While befuddled
underclassmen squeak
out their confusions,
a young
red-tailed hawk
squeaks for attention
from atop
a Harvard Law school
building

My neighborhood

Shops: bank
pharmacy etc

flower bed

apartments

open lawn

city planted trees

over buildings-sunsets
night skies moonphases,
cloud shapes

school
playing
field

apartments

gas station
with planting
tubs

shops

turkeys
hang out
here
and dogs!
and bunnies

home

home

home

deciduous
trees =
sugar maple
Norway maple
ash
locust
basswood
oak

evergreen=
spruce
yew
arborvitae
hemlock

Flower
garden

neighbor saw
a barred
owl here

our
apartment
bldg

flower bed

neighbor
sees:
raccoon
hawks
skunk in
her backyard

⊙ = our
birdfeeder

abandoned house
pigeons hang out on
the roof

chickadees
sparrows
cardinals
titmice
(used to have
house finch
+ pigeons) gray
lots of squirrels!

forsythia where
sparrows hide

VT   NH
NY
CT   RI

My town =
near the Atlantic
early colonial settlement for
fishing, farming, harbor;
now = industry, tech, academics.

W
S ← → N
E

↓ beautiful
sunrises
and moon
rises

If you fly over - flat, covered by trees, one main
river and other open spaces

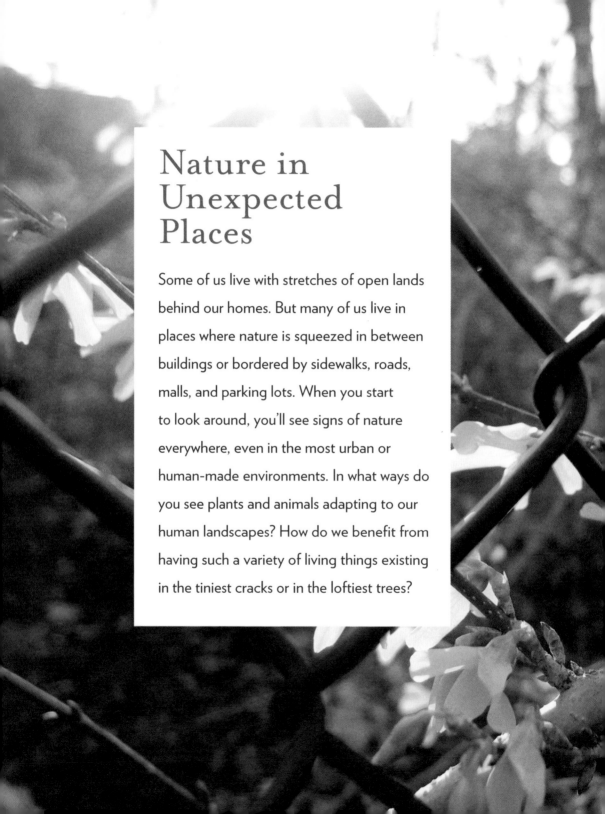

Nature in Unexpected Places

Some of us live with stretches of open lands behind our homes. But many of us live in places where nature is squeezed in between buildings or bordered by sidewalks, roads, malls, and parking lots. When you start to look around, you'll see signs of nature everywhere, even in the most urban or human-made environments. In what ways do you see plants and animals adapting to our human landscapes? How do we benefit from having such a variety of living things existing in the tiniest cracks or in the loftiest trees?

Wherever you are, look for nature around you:

- **Airports**
- **Cemeteries and pocket parks**
- **Golf courses**
- **Bus stops**
- **Parking lots**
- **Schoolyards**
- **Subway platforms**
- **Malls**
- **Hospitals and clinics**
- **Roadsides**
- **Your windowsill**

What Are the Colors of the Day?

Go outdoors or find a window to look out of — what colors do you see? Close your eyes and form an abstract picture of these colors. Try putting your color image on paper with crayons, chalk, colored pencils, markers, or watercolors. How will these colors vary according to the time of day or night, when raining or snowing, or during different seasons?

What would the colors of the seasons look like?

January sleeps dark
February finds one light
that brightens daily

March yawns + melts

April opens to growth

May chases its tail
and won't stop

June's at the
Summit

July becomes the
elder, chasing the
kids away

August blesses
the land

September reminds
us winter is coming

October helps us
forget

November closes shop

December completes
the turning cycle

Jan
Feb
March
April
May
June
July
August
Sept
Oct
Nov
Dec

35

Nature's Moods

What kind of feeling do you get

from different colors on different days?

DISCOVER

Sunrise and Sunset

Have you stopped to watch the sunrise or sunset lately? Noticed how the colors in the sky continually change as the sun comes up in the east, arcs over the sky, then sets in the west? As the light changes, so does bird activity, the smell of the earth and the air, wind velocity, temperature, and even the direction flowers face.

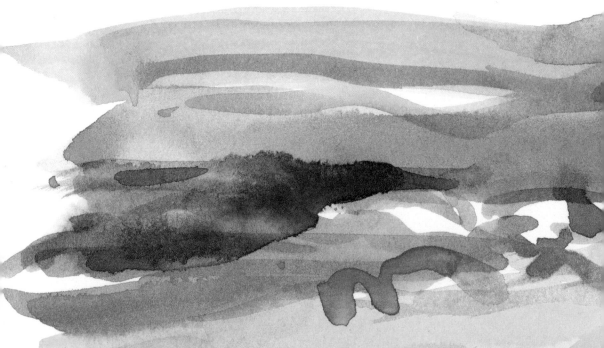

TRY THIS
Note the colors of the sky at sunrise or sunset over the course of a few days or weeks.
Use colored pencils, crayons, or descriptive words to record the colors, dates, and times in a notebook.

Glorious was life . . .
Now I am filled with joy
For every time a dawn
Makes white the sky of night,
For every time the sun goes up
Over the heavens.

— AN IGLULIK ESKIMO SONG OF THE
HUDSON BAY REGION, RECORDED BY
KNUD RASMUSSEN

Did You Know?

The light from the sun is composed of all the colors of the rainbow, all traveling through the atmosphere at varying wavelengths. We usually see these light waves as white because they blend together. During sunrise and sunset, because of the low angle of the sun, mostly the longer wavelengths of red, orange, and yellow colors come through. With pollutants and water vapor in the air, these colors can vary or intensify.

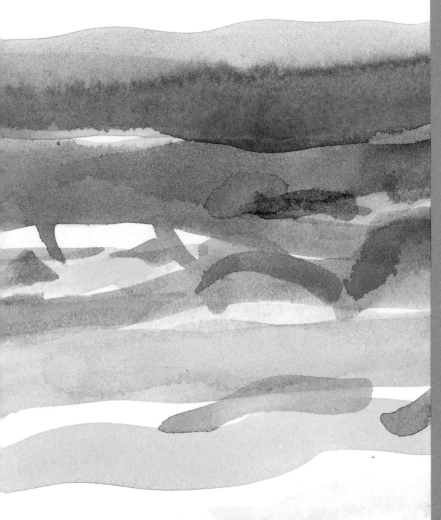

Changing Light

Are the days getting longer or shorter right now?

How much does the length of daylight at different times of year affect what you do or how you feel?

Is there a difference in the quality of the light in fall versus winter?

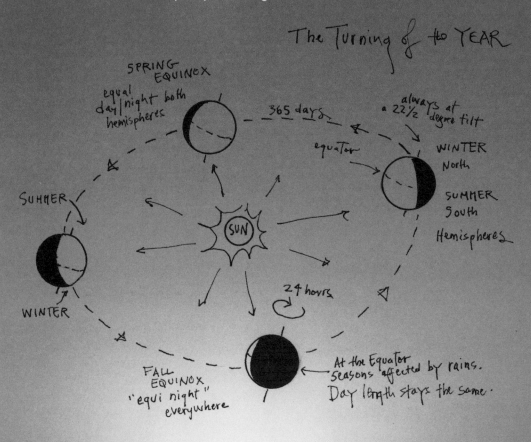

The Turning of the YEAR

SPRING EQUINOX
equal day/night both hemispheres

365 days

always at a 22½ degree tilt

equator

WINTER North

SUMMER South

Hemispheres

SUMMER

SUN

24 hours

WINTER

FALL EQUINOX, "equi night" everywhere

At the Equator Seasons affected by rains. Day length stays the same.

November
envelopes into
dark folds of
quieting colors

The grand October
display
is
over

Mauves
rusts
drizzle
greys
come
on

Look Up

Many artists, musicians, and poets
have been inspired by the sky
and its constantly changing colors,
cloud formations, and weather
moods. Some people who work
outside, such as farmers and
fishermen, learn to read the clouds
to tell what weather is coming.

clouds

When outside, **FEEL** the sun on your face (eyes closed!). **FEEL** the wind, if any. As you are walking, **WONDER** where the wind is coming from and what weather might be coming in. **NOTICE** the clouds: do any of the shapes match what's shown here? Can you learn to read the sky?

10 major cloud shapes to look for

cirrus - wispy

cirrostratus - low + layered

cirrocumulus - little clumps of clouds in rows

altostratus - high + layered

stratus - dense + layered

Clouds change during the day.

nimbostratus - layered, gathering clouds

stratocumulus - dense, layered, piling clouds

Make up your own chart.

Get out from the library books on weather and learn more shapes

cumulus puffy clouds

altocumulus - layers of rolled clouds

cumulonimbus - thunderheads

Did You Know?

Clouds form when water vapor condenses and gathers around particles of sand, pollen, salt, or dust. When enough of these droplets gather together, they become visible as clouds.

Weather Watch

How does weather affect your daily life?

When there is a storm brewing, barometric pressure drops.
Animals can sense this shift in pressure and will adapt
their behavior in preparation. You may spot gulls settling
in groups on the ground, cattle going under trees,
small birds disappearing into shrubbery or under eaves.

What is the weather where you are, right now?
How does the air smell or feel?

WEATHER refers to short-term and localized conditions, whereas CLIMATE involves long-term patterns over a broader area for a longer period. CLIMATE CHANGE is the long-term and lasting change in climate patterns over many years and in many places.

Did You Know?

Red sky at night, sailors delight; red sky at morning, sailors take warning.

Based on experience and observation, many centuries-old weather proverbs are quite predictive. Versions of this proverb appear in the Gospel of Matthew and in Shakespeare's *Venus and Adonis*.

TRY THIS
Write a short poem
or story about a recent
weather event
you have experienced.

This poem is inspired by the ancient blessing poems of
the Celtic Scots living on the Outer Hebrides Islands.

Blessed rain

Blessed soaking rain

Blessed grey blurring green

Blessed cooling

Blessed rain song

Blessed silence of a quiet house

Blessed family safe other places

Blessed dog at my feet sleeping

Blessed time to go nowhere

for a stilled moment

Blessed gardens thanking the summer

for these nourishing rains . . .

—GRANVILLE, VERMONT, JULY 28, 1998

The Night Sky

Depending on how much artificial light there is around you, on a clear night you can see a range of stars, from a few to millions. If the night is dark enough, you might glimpse a shooting star. Sometimes, if you are in the right place, you can even see the northern lights, an eclipse of the moon, or a blazing comet.

Take a night walk.

Let your eyes and mind adjust to being out after dark. How do the smells, sounds, and colors of night differ from those of daytime? Which of your senses feel most alive?

You might want to take a blanket and flashlight and find a dark place where you can sit or lie down and spend some time with the night sky.

Did You Know?

Owls see well at night because they have very large eyes for their body size. Their oval, widely spaced eyes contain many light-sensitive rods that allow for clear long-distance vision under dark conditions. Fox, coyote, and bobcat also have good vision for night hunting.

The Big Dipper
(the Great Bear)

Scorpius
(the Scorpion)

N

Star Map

The night sky is an ancient road map still used today by explorers, sailors, migrating birds, and other animals. Many of the constellations and stars of both the Northern and Southern Hemispheres have the names of characters in the ancient myths and legends of Greek, Roman, and Arabian cultures.

Did You Know? Many songbirds find it safer to migrate at night. If it's a foggy night or

Pleiades in the Constellation Taurus (the Bull)

TRY THIS

Go outside on a dark night

when there is no moonlight (you can try this even in the city), and see if you can find the constellations of Orion, Cassiopeia, the Big Dipper, and Scorpius. You will find them in different places in the sky depending on the season and time of night.

South Pole

The flags of Australia, New Zealand, Papua New Guinea, and Samoa all feature the Southern Cross, a constellation visible in the Southern Hemisphere.

the clouds are low in the sky, you might hear their chirps and cheeps as they call to one another.

The Moon

Like the sun, the moon rises in the east and sets in the west. It always appears to be changing shape, waxing and waning over the 29 days it takes to orbit the earth. It has been repeating this cycle since the dawn of time. What phase is the moon in now?

The side of the moon we see is bright white, as sunlight reflects off its surface. The darker side is the earth's shadow as it passes across the moon, blocking the sun's light.

Full

new   waxing   1st   waxing   waning   last   waning   new
       crescent quarter gibbous   gibbous   quarter   crescent

⟶ 29 days ⟶

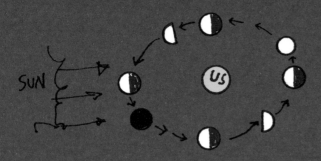

The phases of the moon can be seen on the same days throughout the world. We are turning, and so is the moon.

A total lunar eclipse occurs when the full moon lines up exactly behind the earth and the earth's shadow passes across the moon.

The shadowed moon appears reddish in color because of the way sunlight, coming from the other side of the earth, is filtered and refracted by the earth's atmosphere.

TRY THIS
Have you ever seen a giant moon rising over the eastern horizon? On a full-moon evening in the summer, take a quarter and hold it up to the big rising moon, noting the size of the moon relative to the coin. A few hours later, when the moon is higher in the sky and looks smaller, hold the quarter over the moon again. What do you notice? Even though the full moon seems much larger when it just begins to rise, it isn't — it's an illusion.

Naming the Moon

When you look up at the full moon, do you see a man in the moon? Lovers kissing? A rabbit? Some early peoples had a different name for each month's full moon. These are the names used by the Algonquin people of New England:

JANUARY
Wolf or Hunger Moon

Wolves howl from hunger

FEBRUARY
Snow Moon

Month of the heaviest snows

MARCH
Sap Moon

Sap returns to tree branches from winter storage in roots

APRIL
Grass or Worm Moon

Ground softens, grass shoots show, and worm castings appear in wet soil

MAY
Flower Moon

Spring flowers appear in profusion

JUNE
Strawberry Moon

Time to gather ripening strawberries

JULY
Thunder Moon

Summer storms are frequent and severe

AUGUST
Green Corn Moon

Corn is ready for harvest

SEPTEMBER
Harvest Moon

Crops are harvested

OCTOBER
Hunter's Moon

Animals are hunted, fat from a full summer of eating

NOVEMBER
Beaver Moon

Time to set traps before swamps freeze

DECEMBER
Long Night or Cold Moon

Winter takes hold, and long nights allow the moon to be seen longer

What names would you choose for the moons where you live?

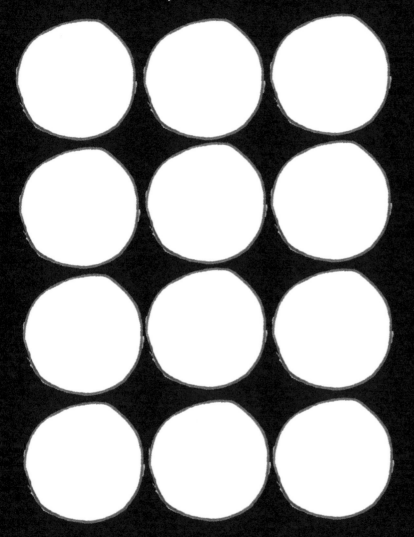

Did You Know?

While the definition of a "blue moon" has evolved over the years, it has come to refer to the second full moon in a calendar month (which is not really blue, but silvery-white, as usual). This second full moon appears every two or three years. Its name comes from the expression "once in a blue moon," which means "very rarely."

In the Garden

Gardens are everywhere. You'll see them along roadsides, in abandoned lots, beside highways, maybe in your yard or your neighbors' yards. What kinds of gardens do you see daily? If you don't have one yourself, would you like to? Start with a window box or a pot on a balcony, and find out if there is a community garden in your neighborhood.

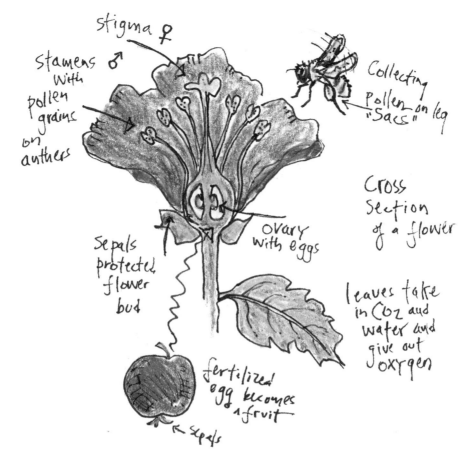

stigma ♀

stamens ♂
with
pollen
grains
on
anthers

Collecting
pollen on leg
"sacs"

Cross
Section
of a flower

Sepals
protected
flower
bud

ovary
with eggs

leaves take
in CO2 and
water and
give out
oxygen

fertilized
egg becomes
a fruit

← sepals

The Pollen Dance

Plants produce fruits, nuts, and seeds that develop from fertilized, expanded eggs inside the ovary of the plant. These eggs are fertilized when pollen from the anther (male part) of the same kind of flower lands on the stigma (female part) of another flower. Some plants depend on the wind to move pollen around, and many depend on insects. The next time you eat a fruit or vegetable or buy flowers, thank a bee, butterfly, spider, or hummingbird.

TRY THIS
Keep your eye out for flowering plants and the insects
that surround them. Which flowers seem to draw the most pollinators? How many pollinators can you find around the same kind of flower?

Wild Plants

There are many plants that no one planted. Some of them we call wildflowers. Some we cultivate for our gardens. But those that creep into our gardens unbidden are labeled as weeds. Weeds (from the Old English word *weod*, meaning "unwanted" or "small") are also the hardy survivors, growing between cement cracks, along sidewalks, and beside railroad tracks. Many came from other countries, arriving in seed bags and grain sacks brought by early colonists.

In earlier cultures and times, wild plants were used as medicines, teas, or foods, as well as for other household purposes such as fabric dyeing and basketmaking.

TRY THIS

Take a closer look at the opportunistic weeds around you. Take photos, make quick sketches, collect and dry them, and identify them later, if you want. Many native plants keep attractive seed pods throughout the winter (like milkweed, dock, burdock, evening primrose, and chicory) and are important food sources for birds, mice, and other small animals.

Try collecting interesting seed pods and making an arrangement of them.

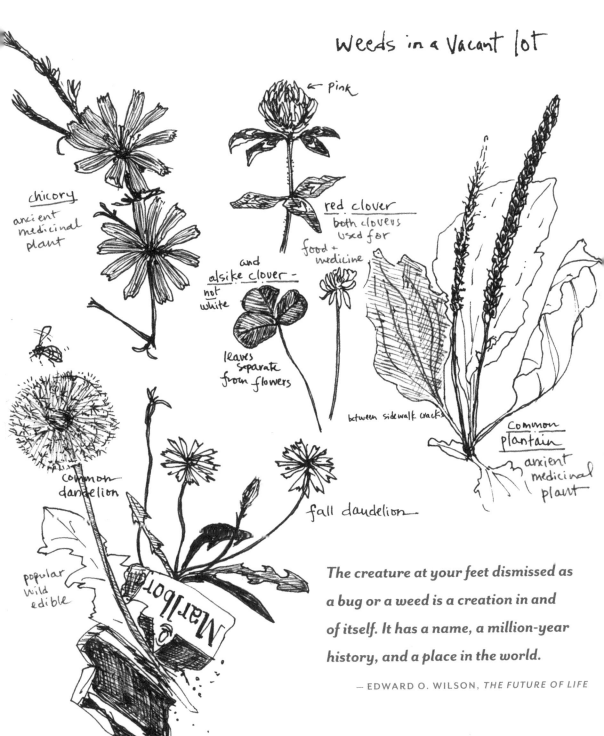

← pink

chicory
ancient
medicinal
plant

red clover
both clovers
used for
food +
medicine

and
alsike clover -
not
white

leaves
separate
from flowers

between sidewalk cracks

common
plantain
ancient
medicinal
plant

common
dandelion

fall dandelion

popular
wild
edible

The creature at your feet dismissed as a bug or a weed is a creation in and of itself. It has a name, a million-year history, and a place in the world.

— EDWARD O. WILSON, *THE FUTURE OF LIFE*

Grasses

A variety of cultivated grasses feed us — wheat, barley, corn, oats, millet, rye, and rice. And wild grasses of all sizes and shapes cover the vast plains of the world. Grasses, with their extensive root systems, help prevent erosion on dunes, hillsides, and riverbanks.

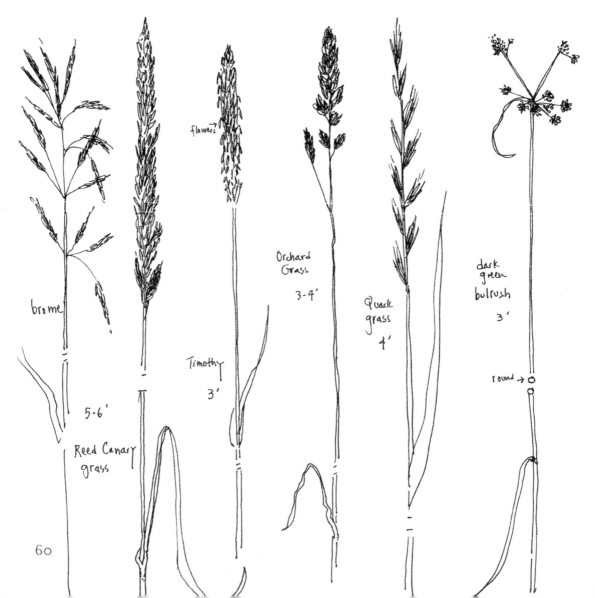

brome

5·6'

Reed Canary grass

flowers

Timothy

3'

Orchard Grass

3-4'

Quack grass

4'

dark green bulrush

3'

round → o

When you walk past a patch of grass, consider the texture, color, smell, even the sound as you swish through it. Who might be hiding in the grass? (Woodchuck, frog, bird?) Who might be eating the grass? (Ladybug, rabbit, grasshopper?)

Carex Crinita
sedge
1–5½'

Redtop or
Bentgrass
10" – 4'

TRY THIS

With string and four sticks, mark off a small section — no more than a square yard — of lawn or other grassy area.

Examine your patch of grass and maybe the soil underneath. Make a list of everything you find.

Return a week or season later and make a new list. What has changed?

No Flowers Here

Have you noticed some of the stranger members of the plant (and fungus) world? Mushrooms growing in damp woods, soft mosses, and ferns in shady places? Instead of having flowers, they reproduce with tiny grainlike spores.

Earthstars
split open and burst
forth spores

Gill mushrooms

Spores
within

mycelium
begin
underground

fruiting body
emerges

moss with
spore capsules

Pore mushrooms

fungi
grow on trees
helping to break
down old wood

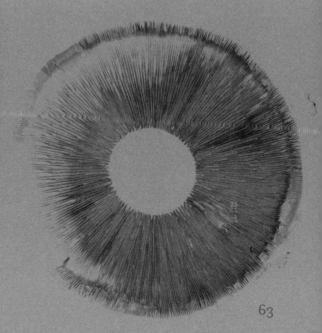

TRY THIS

Make a spore print with a mushroom cap.

Find a mature mushroom and remove the stem. Place the cap, gills down, on a piece of paper or glass. Place a cup or glass upside down over your mushroom to keep breezes away, and let it sit overnight. In the morning, carefully remove the cup and lift the mushroom cap. You should find a "print" like this:

Lichens, a "pioneer" species, grow where nothing else can — in ancient swirls on cold and rocky outcrops, on dry disturbed soil, on rotting logs, wherever the air is clean and unpolluted. The nineteenth-century author Beatrix Potter, who wrote *Peter Rabbit*, researched and discovered that lichens are, in fact, a combination of algae and fungi. Although her research was not recognized during her time, today she is considered to have been an important naturalist as well as artist.

Ruby-throated female hummingbird

The still explosions on the rocks,
the lichens, grow
by spreading, gray, concentric shocks.
They have arranged
to meet the rings around the moon, although
within our memories they have not changed.

— ELIZABETH BISHOP, FROM "THE SHAMPOO"

Did You Know?

Lichens are an important source of food and nesting material for birds and other animals. Also, some fabric dyes come from lichens. Their lovely soft shades of yellow, green, and lavender have colored Scottish tartans for centuries.

Ferns, a nonflowering plant group, have 10,000 species to their name.

Fern leaves unfurl from fiddleheads.

Some, like ostrich ferns, are delicious

when they just emerge in the spring.

Have a look at the underside of a fern frond—

is it covered with spores?

Why! who makes much of a miracle?

As to me, I know of nothing else but miracles,

Whether I walk the streets of Manhattan,

Or dart my sight over the roofs of houses toward the sky,

Or wade with naked feet along the beach, just in the edge of the water,

Or stand under trees in the woods,

Or talk by day with any one I love —

— WALT WHITMAN, FROM "MIRACLES" IN *LEAVES OF GRASS*

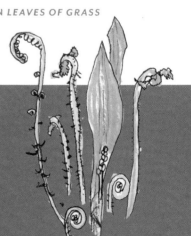

Did You Know?

In New Zealand, the Maori people have used tree ferns for building materials. Ferns can be tiny or gigantic, depending on their species and habitat. Temperate and tropical rain-forest ferns can be as tall as 50 feet.

Trees

Notice the intricate and varied shapes the branches and leaves of trees make against the sky. On sunny afternoons, tree shadows are beautiful thrown across streets and lawns and the sides of buildings. Imagine living without trees. Would it be hotter, colder, windier? Would there be less wildlife?

Do you like being among trees?

Why or why not?

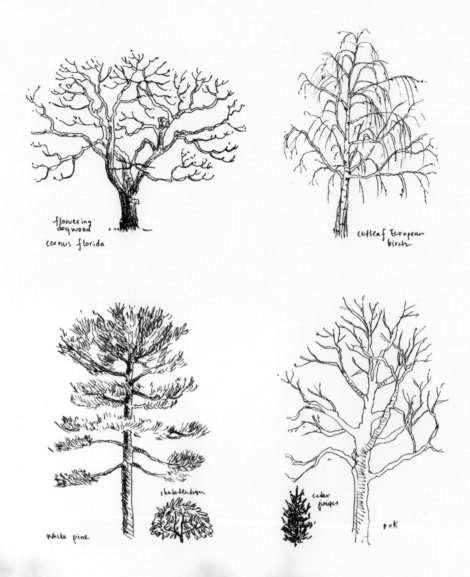

flowering
dogwood
cornus florida

cutleaf European
birch

rhododendron

white pine

cedar
juniper

oak

Can you find tree shapes like these around you?

On your daily route, notice how many different kinds of trees grow where you live.

Do they look old or young, tended or untended?

Deciduous Trees

Deciduous trees generally drop their leaves in autumn to prevent branches from breaking from the weight of snow and keep water from freezing inside the twigs, making them brittle. Sap retreats into the roots for the winter. With warmer spring days, the watery sap — carrying sugars and nutrients — rises again to the twigs, bringing food to buds, leaves, and new growth.

october 17
3:30 pm

red maple

white oak

Did You Know?
The word *tanning* refers to the brown tannic acid in the bark and leaves of oak, among other trees. Leather can be cured and colored using this natural brown chemical.

Fall Leaves

When autumn comes to northern climates, the cooler days signal to the trees that it's time to stop photosynthesizing. Water and the green chemical chlorophyll slowly retreat from the leaves, revealing other chemical colors previously hidden: reds, oranges, purples, yellows. When the leaves fall and dry, these colors fade and the last color, brown, remains until the leaves decay and become new soil. Mulch made from fallen leaves and brush provides protection for many wintering creatures.

Did You Know?
The gingko, a popular city tree, is one of the oldest tree species, a survivor of the last ice age. Called a "living fossil" by Charles Darwin, its fanlike leaves are a beautiful yellow in fall. Gingko nuts are popular in Chinese cuisine.

*Maple leaves
envied by us all,
turning to such
loveliness —
red leaves that fall*

— SHIKO
(JAPANESE POET,
1664 - 1731)

TRY THIS

You can press leaves you have collected

by putting them between sheets of paper towel and placing them under a pile of books. The leaves will become dry enough so you can then tape or glue them onto sheets of paper. Botanists have long used this method for collecting plant specimens. Instead of book piles, they would use plant presses.

irregular margins

no stem

a vine with pretty red fall leaves

Do NOT PRESS Poison Ivy leaves!

Winter Buds

star magnolia buds

TRY THIS
Go on a winter tree-bud walk.
Packed in those small, protective casings are next spring's flowers, leaves, and new twig growth. The magic of trees is they know just when to open those buds (except when Mother Nature brings a late surprise storm!). See if you can notice the day when your favorite tree unlocks its little bud package.

Did You Know?
Trees that lose their leaves in fall actually form next year's buds during the summer, while they still have leaves and the energy to make complex structures.

Winter protected silver maple buds

Spring Flowers

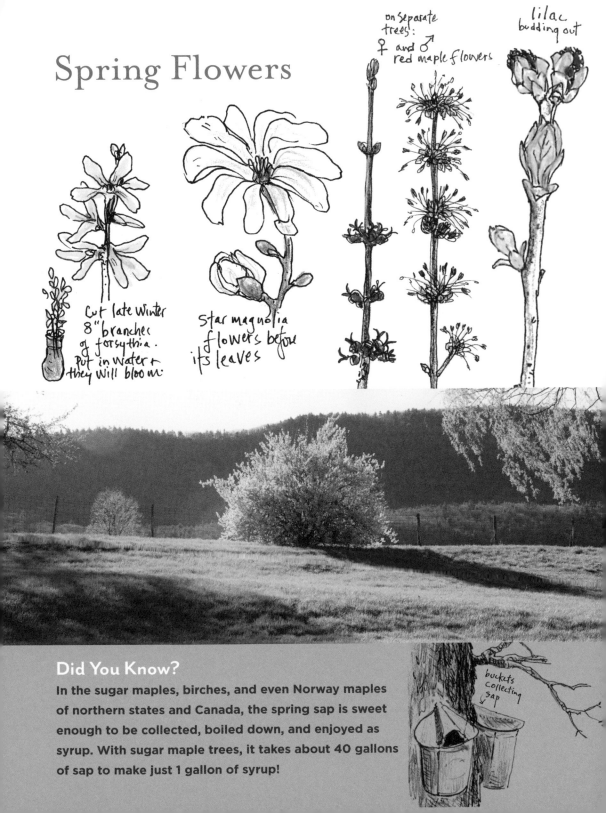

on separate trees:
♀ and ♂ red maple flowers

lilac budding out

Cut late winter 8" branches of forsythia. Put in water + they will bloom.

Star magnolia flowers before its leaves

buckets collecting sap

Did You Know?

In the sugar maples, birches, and even Norway maples of northern states and Canada, the spring sap is sweet enough to be collected, boiled down, and enjoyed as syrup. With sugar maple trees, it takes about 40 gallons of sap to make just 1 gallon of syrup!

Evergreens

Evergreen trees are well adapted to the coldest weather conditions: their sap is thickened with a kind of natural antifreeze so that the needles won't freeze. Thin and tough, the needles also have a waxy coating that helps them conserve water.

Eastern white pine

red pine

5 needles

2 needles

red spruce

balsam fir

sharp points

77

holly

Broadleaf Evergreens

Some trees have flowers rather than cones but do not drop all their leaves before winter. Instead, individual leaves fall throughout the year and are continuously replaced. These are **BROADLEAF EVERGREENS**, most common in the South and in tropical regions but also grown for their beauty in northern regions. In warmer climates, they have adapted by having thick, waxy leaves that absorb more moisture, while in northern climates they have leaves thick enough not to freeze. Some green winter leaves are magnolia, rhododendron, hollies, and ilex.

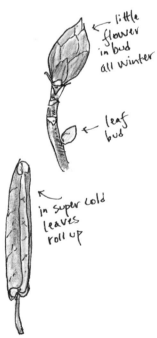

rhododendron
← stay green

← little flower in bud all winter

← leaf bud

in super cold leaves roll up

What percentage
of the trees
around you
do you think are
evergreen?

Did You Know?
Above tree line, spruce and fir trees have adapted
by growing very low to the ground so they won't
be sheered by high winds and cold, blowing snows.
These stunted trees are called *krummholz*,
a German word that means "crooked wood."

Woodland Stroll

What kind of woods or forests
are near you?

Take a walk in the woods, and
try to use all your senses.
In Japan, walking in the woods to
obtain health benefits is called
shinrin-yoku, or "forest bathing";
it calms the body and soul.

See: Let your eyes soften and enjoy the kaleidoscope of images and colors.

Listen: Hear the crunching leaves, chirps of birds and chipmunks, gurgling water.

Touch: Feel the texture of bark, leaf variations, smooth and jagged rocks, and soft moss.

Taste: Bite into an evergreen needle and savor its pungent flavor; breathe in that signature smell we love in incense and Christmas trees.

Smell: Take in the smells of damp woods, pungent mushrooms, rich earth, decaying leaves, spicy ferns. If you scratch a twig of black or yellow birch with your fingernail, it smells like wintergreen. (Crushed wintergreen leaves, which often grow on forest floors of the eastern United States, also smell like — surprise! — wintergreen.)

Did You Know?

In New England, there are many stone walls running through the woods — in fact, there were probably around a quarter-million miles of stone walls in the early twentieth century, made by farmers as they cleared their fields and pastures. Now the landscape is heavily forested again, and many of the farms are gone.

Trees can grow fast if left alone.

How has your landscape changed over the years?

look below

Who Lives in the Trees around You?

Look for nests or tree cavities housing birds, squirrels, raccoons, or even mice.

Standing dead trees are especially good habitat for all sorts of creatures . . .

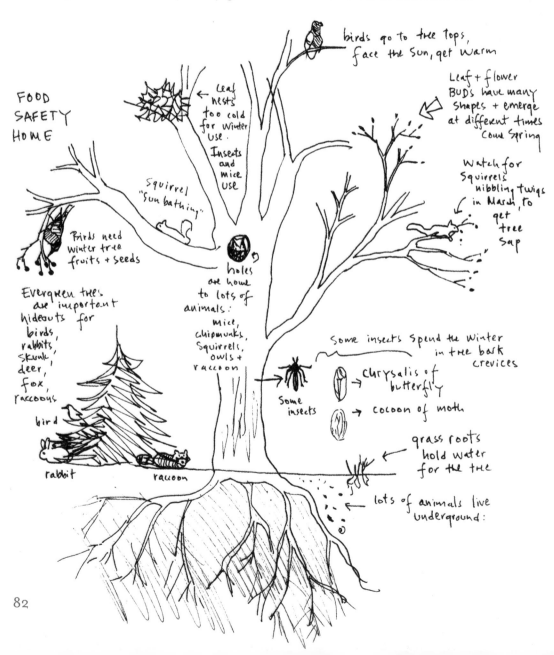

birds go to tree tops, face the sun, get warm

Leaf + flower Buds have many shapes + emerge at different times come spring

Leaf nests too cold for winter use. Insects and mice use

FOOD SAFETY HOME

Watch for squirrels nibbling twigs in March, to get tree sap

Squirrel "Sun bathing"

Birds need winter tree fruits + seeds

Evergreen trees are important hideouts for birds, rabbits, skunk, deer, fox, raccoons

bird

rabbit

raccoon

holes are home to lots of animals: mice, chipmunks, squirrels, owls + raccoon

Some insects spend the winter in tree bark crevices

chrysalis of butterfly

cocoon of moth

Some insects

grass roots hold water for the tree

lots of animals live underground:

Animal Signs

Most animals are secretive, and it may take some time to see any at all. Many only appear at dusk, early dawn, or night. Sometimes all you'll see are the signs they leave behind. What animals live near you?

who am I?

TRY THIS
Take a walk with eyes and ears open. Can you find any of these signs?

- **Tracks in snow or mud**
- **Nibbled shoots of small plants**
- **Nesting sites, lodges, or dens**
- **Scat (droppings)**
- **Fur**
- **Discarded antlers**
- **Bones**

front rear

rabbit hopping

gray squirrel leaping — front rear

bird walking

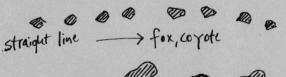

straight line → fox, coyote

people

Some signs are heard and not seen. You might hear an alarm call: the chatters of tree or ground squirrels, a beaver-tail slap, an elk or deer snort, the yips of a raccoon, or the barks of a coyote or fox.

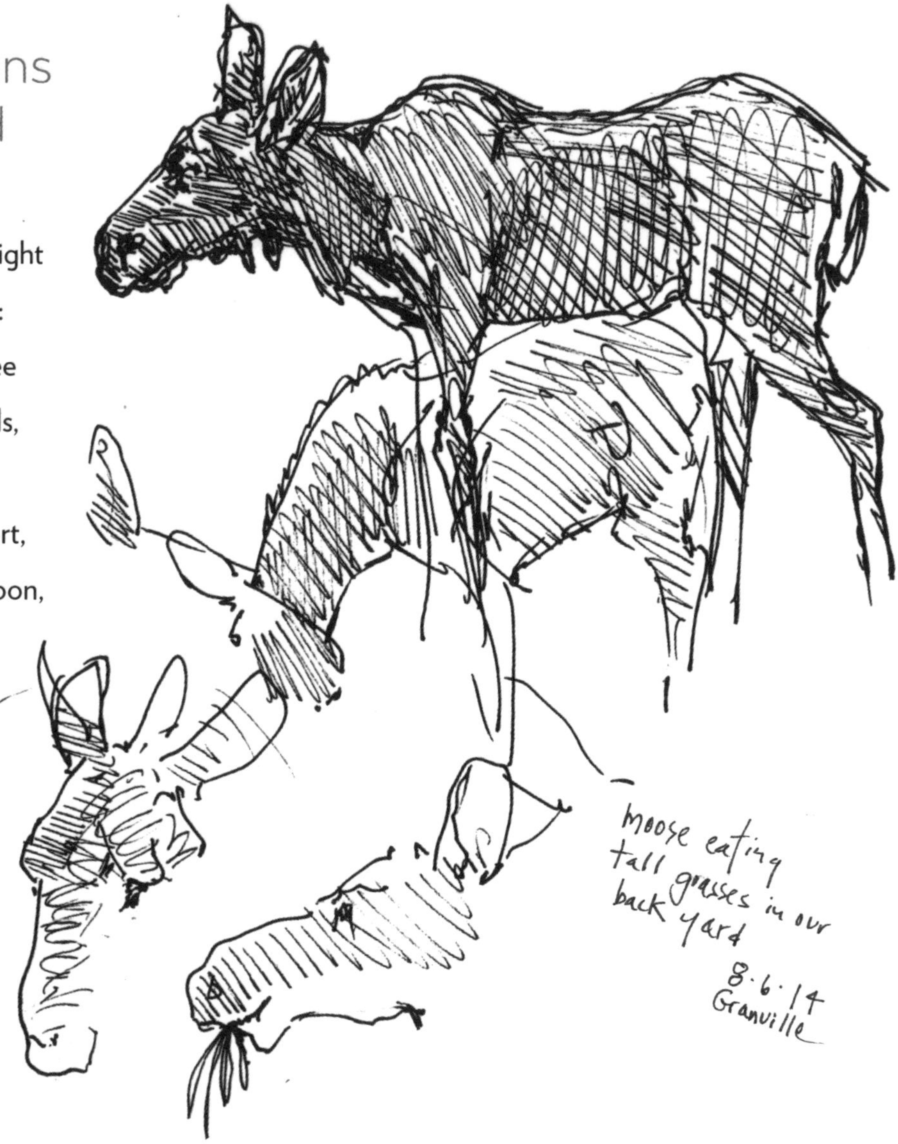

moose eating tall grasses in our back yard
8·6·14
Granville

TRY THIS

Find a quiet place by a river, in a field, in the woods. Settle down and close your eyes. Listen. What do you hear? **Rustling . . . chattering . . . chewing . . . snorting . . . twittering . . . wind . . . an airplane . . . people? Open your eyes and try to find the sources. If you are lucky enough to see an animal, be still and quiet and watch for a while. Can you be so watchful that the animal watches you?**

How do animals adapt to the place where they live?

Members of the canine family, such as wolves, foxes, and coyotes, have adapted to many different and sometimes harsh environments.

Kit fox
of the desert
Large ears to release
heat; small and slender
26 - 34"

red fox
adapted to
suburban and
farmland
habitats
35 - 45"

Coyotes
have moved
East from
Western grasslands
and prairies, becoming
larger in size
41 - 52"

Arctic fox
Thick fur, compact
body, short ears, all to
conserve heat. Color changes
from winter white to summer
dark brown 29 - 36"

Gray wolf
Heavy set body,
camouflaged for
northern
wilderness 3 - 6'

On the Wing

Birds have always fascinated people. Although the daily activities of some birds can be readily seen, whether it's flying, feeding, being fed, preening, singing, or nest building, their ways are magical as well as mysterious. They appear as part of our lives, and then they fly off. We still know very little about the behavior patterns of many bird species.

Hope is the thing with feathers —

That perches in the soul —

And sings the tune without the words —

And never stops — at all —

— EMILY DICKINSON

Snowy owl
1·27

wing tips on airplanes today

large birds soaring outer wings up

AIRPLANE DESIGNS mimic birds' hollow bones, angled wings, and physics of flight.

MOTORCYCLE HELMETS copy the shape of woodpecker heads.

THERE ARE NEARLY 10,000 SPECIES OF BIRDS worldwide, and 645 species breed in North America.

MANY BIRDS can sleep with one eye open. They may even sleep on the wing!

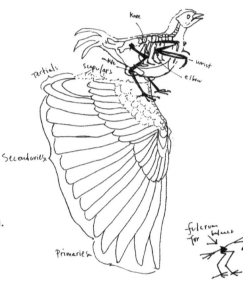

knee

wrist

elbow

ankle

scapulars

tertials

Secondaries

Primaries

fulcrum for levers

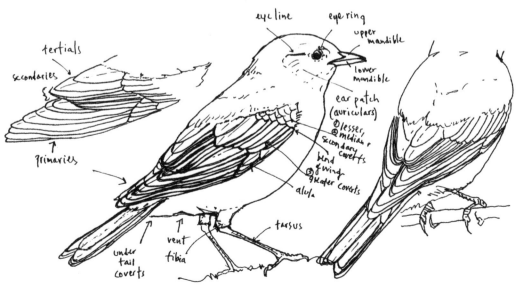

eye line

eye ring

upper mandible

lower mandible

ear patch (auriculars)

①lesser, ②median secondary coverts

bend of wing

greater coverts

alula

tarsus

tertials

secondaries

primaries

under tail coverts

vent

tibia

Are you ever awakened by birdsong early in the morning? Instead of rolling over, listen for a minute. Do you hear the same songs each morning? How about in the evening and the middle of day? Can you see any of the birds as they sing?

Try choosing one kind of bird, or even one individual bird, to watch closely from day to day.

What are its particular habits?

Migrants Passing Through

The vast seasonal migrations of animals have long captured our curiosity and wonder. For a long time, people didn't know where migrating animals went in winter. As late as the sixteenth century, it was thought that swallows hibernated in caves or at the bottoms of ponds. With modern technology, our understanding of migratory patterns continues to expand.

Did You Know?

The longest two-way annual migration is made by the arctic tern, flying up to 11,000 miles between the Arctic, where it nests, and Antarctica.

The longest distance flown (nonstop) relative to a small body size is 500 miles by the ruby-throated hummingbird, across the Caribbean Gulf.

Adult salmon can migrate as far as 1,800 miles inland from the mouth of Alaska's Yukon River on the Bering Sea to the smallest interior freshwater streams in Canada's Yukon Territory.

Some dragonflies migrate and can fly at speeds over 34 miles per hour.

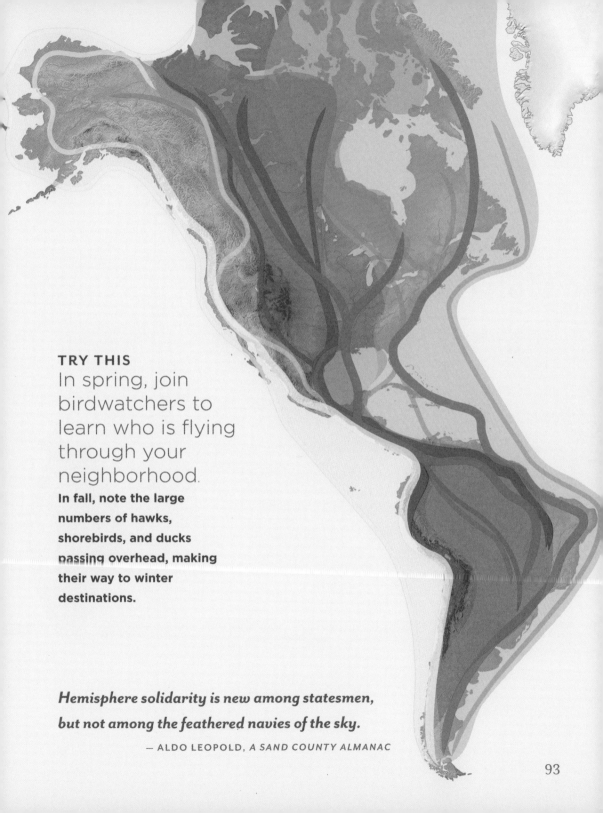

TRY THIS

In spring, join birdwatchers to learn who is flying through your neighborhood. In fall, note the large numbers of hawks, shorebirds, and ducks passing overhead, making their way to winter destinations.

Hemisphere solidarity is new among statesmen, but not among the feathered navies of the sky.

— ALDO LEOPOLD, *A SAND COUNTY ALMANAC*

93

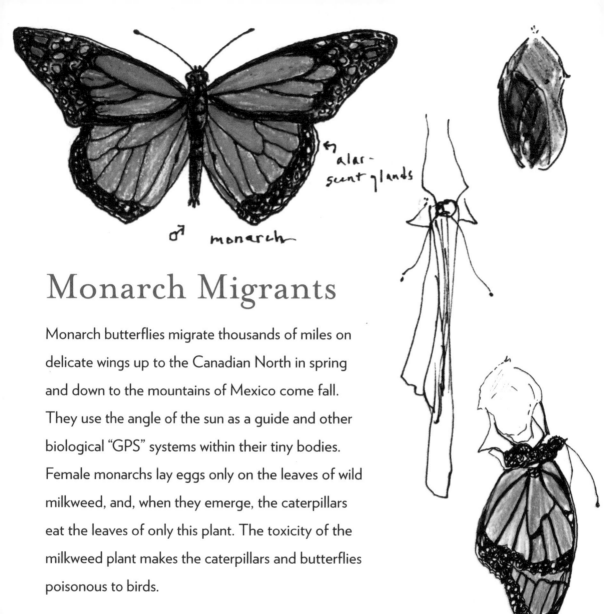

alar-scent glands

♂ monarch

Monarch Migrants

Monarch butterflies migrate thousands of miles on delicate wings up to the Canadian North in spring and down to the mountains of Mexico come fall. They use the angle of the sun as a guide and other biological "GPS" systems within their tiny bodies. Female monarchs lay eggs only on the leaves of wild milkweed, and, when they emerge, the caterpillars eat the leaves of only this plant. The toxicity of the milkweed plant makes the caterpillars and butterflies poisonous to birds.

TRY THIS
Look for monarchs around fields where milkweed may be growing. These creatures are thought to be named by early settlers after King William III, Prince of Orange. Their orange and black colors are distinctive. When you see one, you might want to report your sighting to a nature center and join with other citizen scientists in monitoring the health of this species. You might even plant some milkweed in your backyard.

stages of
metamorphosis

Insect Beauty ant

Insects are the most diverse group of animals on the planet; in fact, they make up about 80 percent of the world's species! Around a million insect species have been described, and scientists believe there are millions more yet to be discovered. Throughout history, naturalists have collected insect specimens not only because of their amazing beauty and variation in color, shape, and size, but to learn about their habitats and how they survive in vastly different conditions. Insects are important pollinators, as well as food sources for other animals.

ctenucha moth

x 1⅛ common sulphur

x 1 cabbage white

♂ Spring azure x 1

♀

Isabella moth

underwing moth

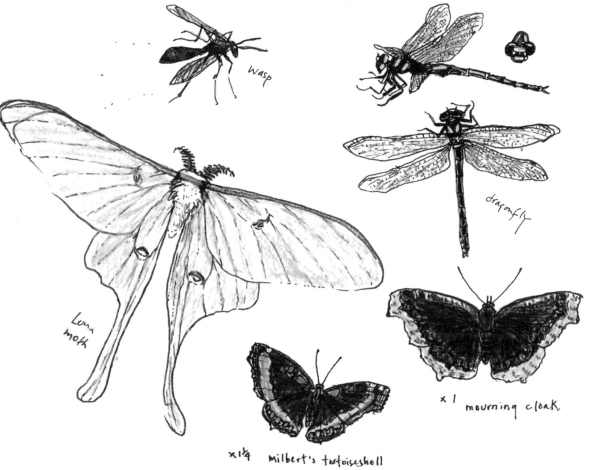

wasp

dragonfly

Luna moth

x 1¼ milbert's tartoiseshell

x 1 mourning cloak

Did You Know?
Insects breathe through tiny holes along the sides of their bodies called spiracles.

Spiders and Their Kin

Different kinds of spiders weave different styles of webs, many of which can be stunningly beautiful. Even in a tiny area, several kinds of spiders may coexist. And most are friendly to us, catching many of the insects we don't like.

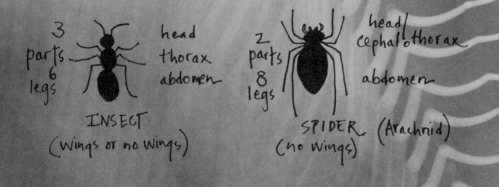

3 parts
6 legs
head
thorax
abdomen

INSECT
(wings or no wings)

2 parts
8 legs
head/ cephalothorax
abdomen

SPIDER (Arachnid)
(no wings)

TRY THIS
Explore for spiderwebs. Early in the morning can be best, when dew and low sunlight reveal intricate fibers spun on streetlights, gates, and branches, in the cups of flowers, or low in the grass. If you are patient, you might see a spider wrap its prey!

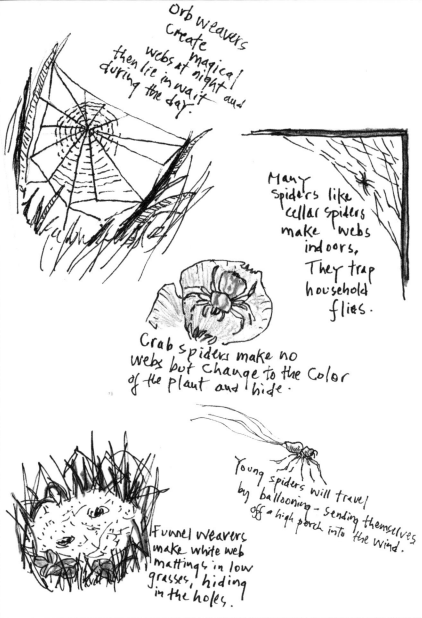

Orb weavers create magical webs at night and then lie in wait during the day.

Many spiders like cellar spiders make webs indoors, They trap household flies.

Crab spiders make no webs but change to the color of the plant and hide.

Young spiders will travel by ballooning - sending themselves off a high porch into the wind.

Funnel weavers make white web mattings in low grasses, hiding in the holes.

Spider relatives include crabs, daddy longlegs, and ticks.

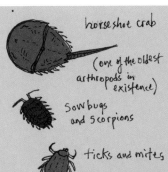

horseshoe crab

(one of the oldest arthropods in existence)

sow bugs and scorpions

ticks and mites

The web of life is much more complicated than even the most beautiful spider silk, and every bug is both a hero and a villain.

—SALLY ROTH,
THE OLD FARMER'S ALMANAC, 2013

Hidden Creatures

Let's not forget those who cannot run or fly. These include the cold-blooded amphibians and reptiles. On a warm day, you may find a snake sunning on a rock, a turtle on a log, or a lizard on a boardwalk. When winter comes, they find a protected place and go into a deep sleep. Some, like wood frogs, even freeze (and thaw out again in spring)!

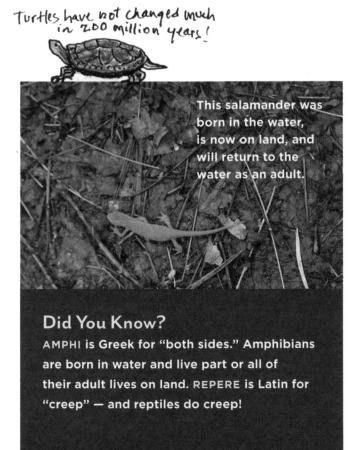

Turtles have not changed much in 200 million years!

This salamander was born in the water, is now on land, and will return to the water as an adult.

Did You Know?

AMPHI is Greek for "both sides." Amphibians are born in water and live part or all of their adult lives on land. REPERE is Latin for "creep" — and reptiles do creep!

WOOD FROG
"Squuck. squuck" like a duck

TRY THIS

Frogs and toads are renowned singers. On a warm night in late March or early April, find a woodland area beside a swamp, shallow pool, pond, or lake.

Sit quietly and listen.

Invisible choristers will soon start up their lusty mating calls. Phantoms of the night, they are guaranteed to enchant you!

PEEPER TREEFROG

high "peep. peep" peeping calls

Fish Tales

The first fish evolved in the oceans about
530 million years ago. Since they breathe
through gills, fish have always lived only in
water, whether fresh, salt, or brackish.

Find a place where someone is fishing, or join someone you know who fishes.

Find out what they are catching and how they are doing it. Some people find fishing meditative. Watch the patience and focused concentration that comes to people who fish.

Ocean Life

The waters of the Pacific, Atlantic, Arctic, and Indian Oceans and the adjoining seas cover about 70 percent of our planet. When you take a deep breath, consider this: In the process of photosynthesis, small surface-living aquatic plants called phytoplankton release oxygen into the ocean. Half the earth's oxygen comes from these tiny organisms (the rest from photosynthesizing land plants).

But where does all that salt come from? It comes from the land: rainwater erodes rock and carries the dissolved salts and minerals to the rivers and streams, which then carry them to the ocean.

Have you ever tasted the salty ocean?

Do fish have ears?

No, but they do have tiny pores on either side of their bodies that detect vibrations and pressure changes.

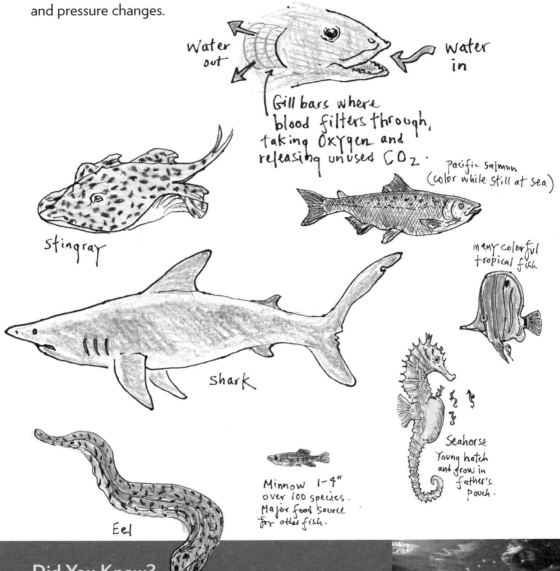

Water out

water in

Gill bars where blood filters through, taking Oxygen and releasing unused CO_2.

Pacific salmon (color while still at sea)

stingray

many colorful tropical fish

shark

Seahorse Young hatch and grow in father's pouch.

Eel

Minnow 1-4" over 100 species. Major food source for other fish.

Did You Know?

The American eel (a kind of fish) makes a unique long-distance journey from streams and lakes to the open ocean to spawn. Because they can absorb oxygen through their gills and skins, they can move on land, traveling over wet grass or mud to the next water source.

Near and Far from Shore

Whales and their relatives are all mammals of the sea, but their survival has been threatened due to overhunting. Now, with strict management and the popularity of whale-watching tours, many populations of whales, seals, walruses, dolphins, and porpoises are recovering.

Humpback whales are the most acrobatic, for being 50-60 feet long. Their annual migration is lengthy, from the West Indies to Greenland

Beluga whales, at 11-13 feet, are white to hide in the ice floes from predators. Native peoples still can harvest a percentage.

The Maine Rocky Coast

"The lasting pleasures of contact with the natural world are not reserved for scientists but are available to anyone who will place (herself) under the influence of earth

sea

and

sky

and their amazing life."

last sentence in Rachel Carson's *The Sense of Wonder* who was a Maine resident

harbor seals

barnacles

rockweed

knotted wrack

periwinkles

dog whelk

Common loon

kelp

limpets

blood star

rock crab

Common Eider

Your Watershed

All land on earth is part of a watershed.
A watershed is the area of land from which
rain collects and runs down into a body
of water. The water flows down streams
and rivers to larger rivers and lakes, through
marshlands, and eventually out to an ocean.
The mighty Mississippi begins in northern
Minnesota as a tiny rivulet 2,300 miles from
the Gulf of Mexico.

Do you know where
your household water
comes from?

This is a dynamic space, a ceaseless mutability awash with tides, with the flowing animation of birds, a confrontation of clouds and light, a zest of winds, a primal soundscape, bracing, elemental, vital.

— JOHN THRELFALL, *BETWEEN THE TIDES*

TRY THIS

Consider the shape of the landscape around you. What streams and lakes and rivers are nearby, and how are they connected? What direction are they flowing? How do you suppose they get to the sea?

The Water Cycle

Water is constantly being recycled, from land to sky and back down again.

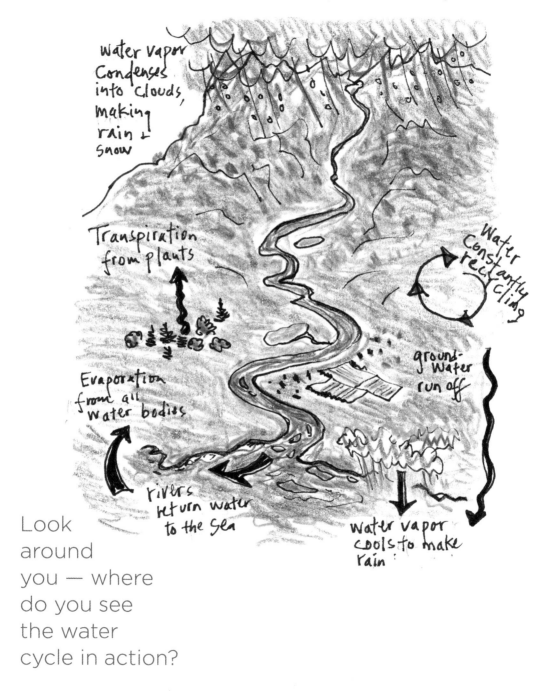

Water vapor condenses into clouds, making rain & snow

Transpiration from plants

Water constantly recycling

ground-water run off

Evaporation from all water bodies

rivers return water to the sea

water vapor cools to make rain

Look around you — where do you see the water cycle in action?

Did You Know?

About 100 million billion gallons of water pass through the earth's gigantic water cycle each year. Ice, rain, oceans, rivers, clouds, lakes, groundwater, reservoirs, plants, animals — all part of a closed cycle. There is no new water being created. The water you drink today may have been drunk by dinosaurs.

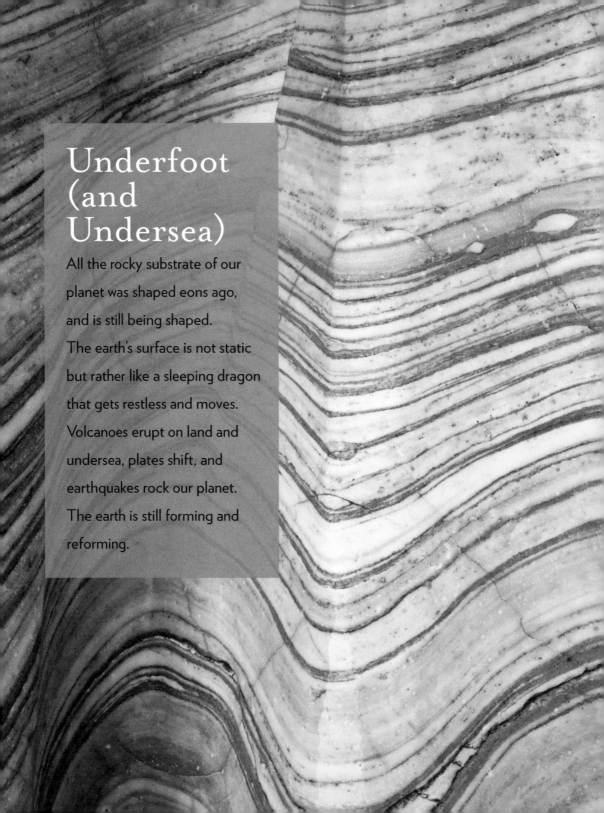

Underfoot (and Undersea)

All the rocky substrate of our planet was shaped eons ago, and is still being shaped. The earth's surface is not static but rather like a sleeping dragon that gets restless and moves. Volcanoes erupt on land and undersea, plates shift, and earthquakes rock our planet. The earth is still forming and reforming.

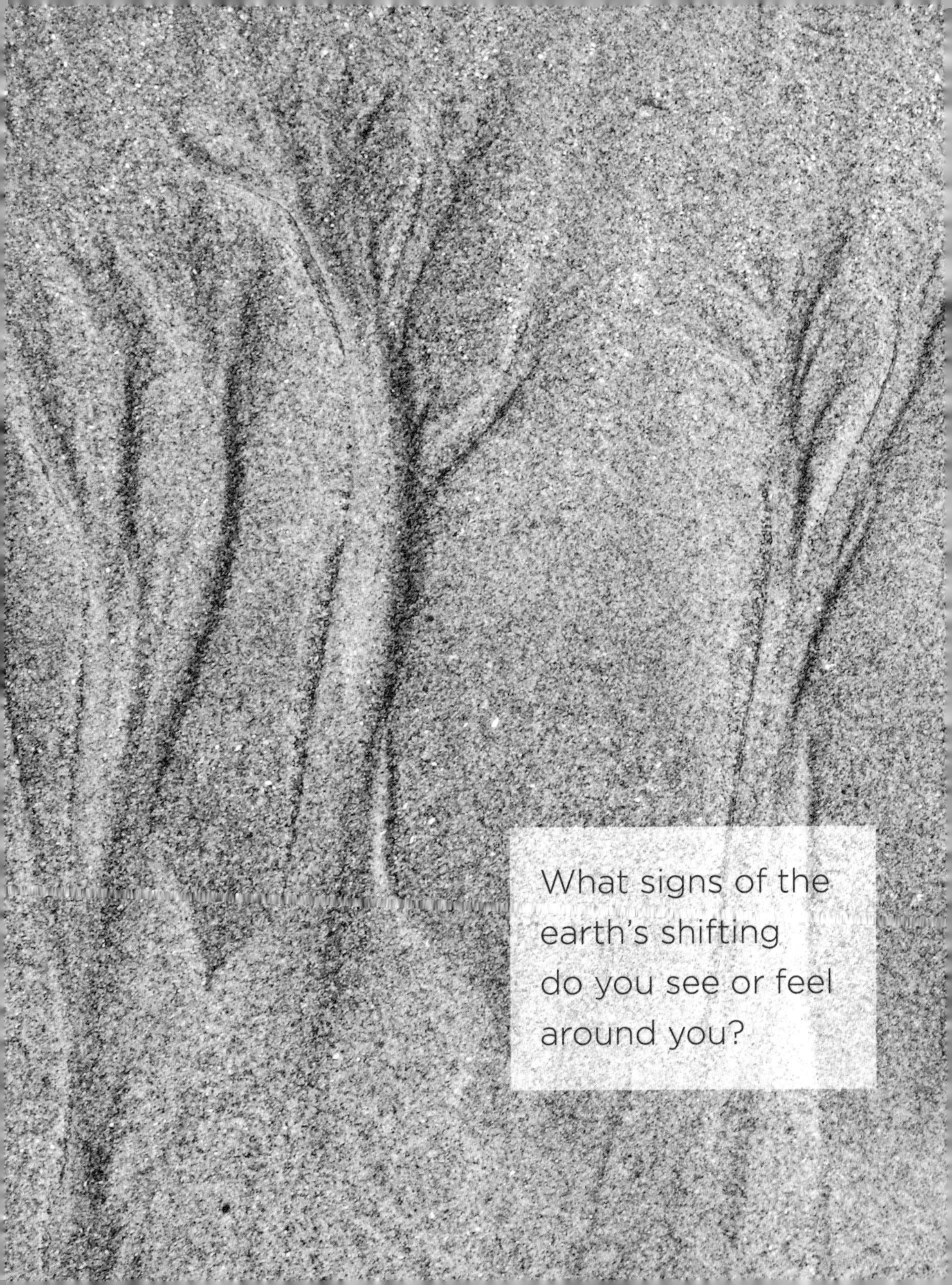

What signs of the
earth's shifting
do you see or feel
around you?

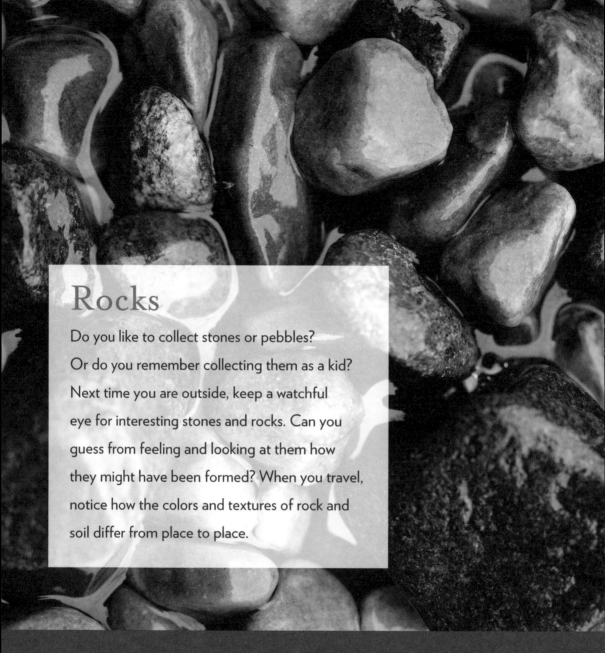

Rocks

Do you like to collect stones or pebbles?
Or do you remember collecting them as a kid?
Next time you are outside, keep a watchful
eye for interesting stones and rocks. Can you
guess from feeling and looking at them how
they might have been formed? When you travel,
notice how the colors and textures of rock and
soil differ from place to place.

Did You Know?

Millions of years ago, petroleum was formed from the remains of plants and
animals that were buried and then transformed by intense heat and pressure.
The ancient people of China and the Mediterranean used unrefined petroleum
in various ways. (*Petra* is the Latin word for rock; *oleum* is the Latin word for oil.)

Igneous rocks are formed from hot lava thrown from a volcano or magma deep in the earth.

Cooled rapidly above ground, this material becomes BASALT, fine-grained and nearly black.

Cooled slowly underground, it becomes coarse-grained GRANITE.

Metamorphic rocks are formed when previously existing rock is changed by heat or immense pressure.

SLATE is formed from compressed mud and clay.

MARBLE is metamorphic limestone.

Sedimentary rocks are layered rocks formed from the fragments of older rocks that have eroded or weathered into sediment like sand or mud. The sediment gets layered and compacted, and you can often see individual minerals or pieces of the older rock within the new one. Occasionally you can find fossilized remains of plants and animals trapped between layers of sedimentary rock. This is also where fossil fuels are found, in the forms of coal, tar sands, shale oil, natural gas, and crude oil.

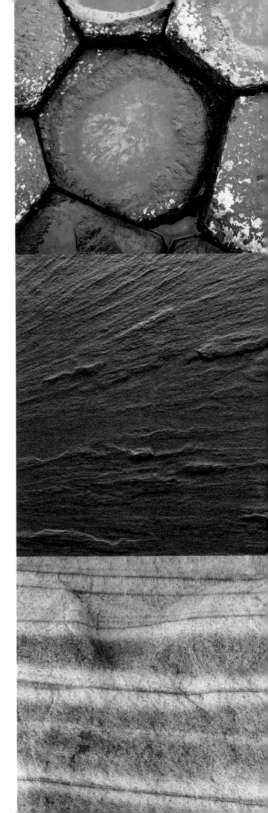

Once in a lifetime, if one is lucky, one so
merges with sunlight and air and running
water that whole eons, the eons that
mountains and deserts know, might pass in a
single afternoon without discomfort.

— LOREN EISELEY,
THE IMMENSE JOURNEY

Shale and Sedimentary
rock road cut

West Virginia

When you take a walk or drive, look carefully at the landscape around you.

Do you see hills or mountains or flat river valleys? Are there open road cuts where you can see the differing layers of rock? The origins of these features go all the way back to the formation of our planet some 4.6 billion years ago and were shaped by tremendous and ancient pressures within the earth.

Did You Know?

Many recognizable land formations were once under water or ice. Fossilized sea creatures have been found near the peaks of the Himalayas!

Meanwhile, deep in the ocean, diverse species make their homes beside rocky shelves, ridges, and ancient ocean craters, scars of an ever-shifting planet.

CONNECT

A Place to Observe through the Seasons

Find a quiet, accessible place you can visit often to watch nature through the seasons and years. The beauty of finding one place (or several) is that it becomes familiar enough that you know what to look for, and yet it is always different. You can spend small amounts of time there between commitments, or you can plan to spend several hours there. The time of day, weather, season, your mood, and who you are with will vary your experience of a place every time you visit, and you'll always find something interesting to watch, write about, or draw.

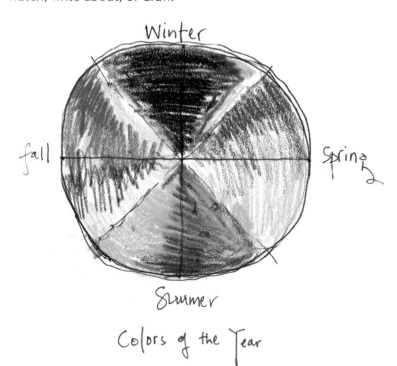

Colors of the Year

...ber !
...hain
...pm

...the ...ing pumpkin smell
...flowing sounds
of oak leaves
dropping
and then a

Keeping an Observation Journal

Next time you take an excursion into the natural world, whether to a place you like to visit regularly or to a new place, you might want to take a blank book in which you can begin keeping ongoing observations.

If you don't want to draw, you can write in different colored inks, use stamps, or mount pressed leaves and flowers on your journal pages with tape. You can even use photographs and news clippings.

Here is one example of how to set up your journal:

Date
Place
Time
weather   sky picture
Sunrise
Sunset
moon phase
hear / see
a few written reflections on the day

N
W   E
S

Drawings/ Writings/ observations:
Just walk about, getting used to the place
① what's on the ground
② Beside you
③ Above you

and so on

Even you are so welcome in your golden glow along the bricks

Tuesday April 18
A Cambridge Spring Walk
1:50 - 3:30 pm
(Flung off all the indoor stuff
to get out - endless e·mails etc...)

Sun · balmy · lovely
people out w/out coats...
Workers scraping house paint
everywhere

Cardinal strong call

Up Lancaster Street

Sitting on a stool w/
Sun on my back - moving
up into North of sky
Calm sitting
waning moon
Sunrise = 5:58 am 13½ hrs
Sunset = 7:29 pm light!

blue sky
Sun
little clouds

Norway maple
flowers out

late
winter
shadows

honeysuckle

dogwood

carinia

Forsythia
gorgeous

Cabbage
butterfly

huge bees
are out &
about!

x2
inspecting
my paper

marsh colors

High Pines
3 pm   Duxbury Beach w/ CWL (as in Chris Leahy)   Sept. 13 '07

What did you see today?

What details of nature caught your attention or made you curious?

January 9
Tower view @ Mt Auburn
2:30 pm
Sunny · 30°s
☾ last quarter moon
Sunrise = 7:13 am *
Sunset = 4:30 pm
*1st day of one minute earlier rise since June 11!
9 hrs 17 min light

Here are the haunts of coyote and rabbit
hawk and tree shadows
with moon full rising 4:30 on Jan. 2

red-bellied woodpecker

hear sounds of
chickadee
robin
red bellied woodpecker
traffic
sirens

Did You Know?
From 1803 to 1806, Meriwether Lewis and William Clark were hired to lead the Corps of Discovery with the specific charge to map, draw, and carefully record their observations. They believed their journals to be as important as their guns and swords. Today, these journals provide accounts of the 178 plants and 122 animals they observed.

Small Wonders

Brief images of nature can help stitch our days together. They can lift us above the humdrum of what we are doing and take us, if just for a moment, out into the vastness of nature. These brief images urge us beyond ourselves. Like little pearls on a strand, they can be noticed and pocketed for whenever you need them.

Oct 20
4 pm or so
A STORY:
Looked up
+ out
Healthworks
Window —
rt hawk
after
pigeons
on the roof

sneaky bandit
on a snowy night
Feb 7

Nature over the Kitchen Sink

Tune in to the presence of miracles, and in an instant, life can be transformed into a dazzling experience, more wondrous and exciting than we could even imagine.

DEEPAK CHOPRA
THE SPONTANEOUS FULFILLMENT OF DESIRE

Find a way to pass your small wonders on to friends, relatives, or colleagues. See if you can start an informal exchange.

- **Exchange text messages**
- **Send pictures by phone**
- **Send pictures by post**
- **Post to a website or blog**
- **Find out if you can use a public bulletin board at a coffee shop or co-op, and invite everyone to post their notes or pictures.**

TRY THIS
Start collecting notes, photos, or drawings of small wonders.
They can be brief, grand, consoling, funny, or they can simply catch you by surprise. How do these connections make you feel?

Solace and Connection

Professor E. O. Wilson coined the term *biophilia*, meaning "love of the living world," to describe the instinctive bond between humans and nature. We need nature; nature is part of us, and we are part of it, whether we are conscious of it or not.

Scientists have long studied the effects of nature and natural images on mental and physical health. Where have you found images of nature that help calm and comfort you? Where can you be reminded of them when you need them?

Wed Oct 18 ~ 12-3pm

Sarah comes over and we go for a walk/catch up in the now glorious · orange glowing Mount Auburn. Sarah gets a phone call from Leigh saying that Tim now has stage four cancer that has spread.
 We talk, watching the yellow leaves cascading slowly down.
 I know better and better that despite our griefs, this seasonal world continues turning — and will continue.
 A source of some comfort.
 Together, in silence, we walk shuffling through the sifting leaves, hearing geese honking as they pass over.

The best remedy for those who are afraid, lonely, or unhappy is to go outside. . . . I firmly believe that nature brings solace in all troubles.

— ANNE FRANK, *THE DIARY OF ANNE FRANK*

A Walking Meditation

Roaming outside, even if only for 20 minutes, can often make you feel better, calmer, less anxious than if you had stayed indoors and checked off one more chore. Historically, successful hunters, explorers, field scientists, and artists of all kinds have had to slow their minds to focus and pay full attention to the subject at hand, whether that's the deer in the woods or the music on the page.

There is no Wi-Fi in the forest, but I promise you will find a better connection.

— ON A POSTCARD OF A PACIFIC NORTHWEST FOREST

In moments of stillness and acute quietness, when the noisy mind is devoid of the chaotic business of thinking, an awareness of another dimension reveals itself. It is a dimension of union; the viewer and that being viewed are one. It is the ending of isolation. — DEL WYNN, *ACK POETICALLY*

Did You Know?

The well-known primatologist Dr. Jane Goodall would sit for hours in the Gombe game preserve in Tanzania, waiting and watching for the chimpanzees she was studying. Henry David Thoreau took two years to sit and watch the nature around his small cabin. To be a creative thinker, whether artist or scientist, child or adult, we all need time for quiet reflection when the mind and heart can grow calm and we can see things a bit more clearly.

TRY THIS
Find time for a quiet walk anywhere outdoors, for as long as you have time.

Try walking without taking anything along.

Focus only on the nature you see around you, and try to keep your mind from wandering. Notice leaf shapes, colors of sunlight, clouds passing, birds moving about. Listen for the wind or a bird call. Breathe deeply. Notice the slowing of your heartbeat. When you get home, see if you can carry this lightness of spirit into what comes next.

Nature and Art

Nature has been a vital source for
creative inspiration of all kinds going
back as far as 17,000 years ago to
the early Paleolithic paintings on the
cave walls of Lascaux, France. The work
of writers, painters, sculptors, crafts-
people, architects, dancers, musicians,
and other artists the world over
is influenced by the natural world.

Which artists do you admire who use nature as inspiration?

TAKE A LOOK AT:

- Monet's water lilies and haystacks

- Georgia O'Keefe's flowers and desert scenes

- Winslow Homer's seascapes

- Calder's mobiles

- The photography of Edward Weston and Ansel Adams

- The delicate natural forms captured by Japanese brush painters

"We often forget that we are nature. Nature is not something separate from us. So when we say that we have lost our connection to nature, we've lost our connection to ourselves."

— ANDY GOLDSWORTHY,
BRITISH ENVIRONMENTAL ARTIST
AND PHOTOGRAPHER

'28. 07

Make a date with yourself to visit an art museum.
Note the paintings, the pottery, fabrics and weavings, and sculptures that express some connection with nature. Do any of them make you want to see the places or things they depict?

Are you inspired to create your own art from nature?

Music

Many composers are inspired by the natural world. Vivaldi's
The Four Seasons, Tchaikovsky's *Swan Lake*, and Copland's
Appalachian Spring are just a few of the many classical pieces
that might transport you into nature.

Spring song
of the wood thrush
is magical

Did You Know?

The contemporary composer John Luther Adams has long created
music deeply rooted in the natural world. He has created musical
pieces that mimic birdsong, for example. And in 2009, he translated
geophysical data streams into an environment of sound and light in
an installation called *The Place Where You Go to Listen*.

TRY THIS
Listen to the work of any musician influenced by the natural world.

What does their music make you think and feel?

What images or memories does it inspire?

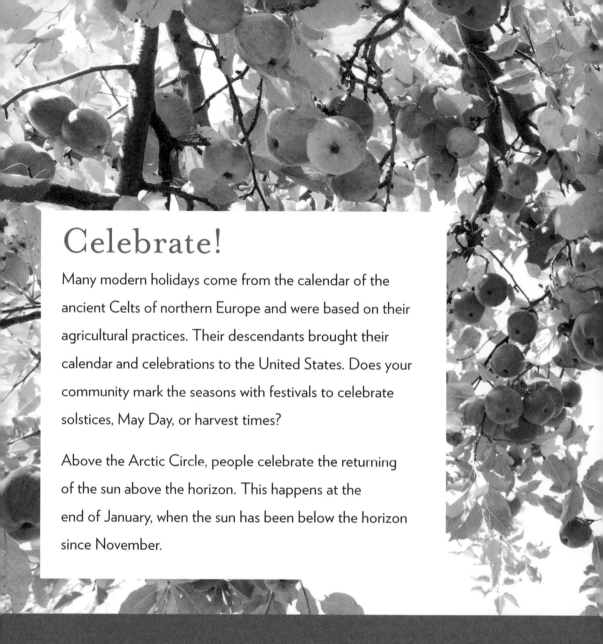

Celebrate!

Many modern holidays come from the calendar of the ancient Celts of northern Europe and were based on their agricultural practices. Their descendants brought their calendar and celebrations to the United States. Does your community mark the seasons with festivals to celebrate solstices, May Day, or harvest times?

Above the Arctic Circle, people celebrate the returning of the sun above the horizon. This happens at the end of January, when the sun has been below the horizon since November.

Did You Know?

The word *Easter* comes from the names of ancient goddesses of spring, fertility, and dawn: Ishtar, Astarte, Eostre, Eos. Halloween (meaning "holy eve") came out of an early Christian adaptation of the most important festival of the Celtic agricultural year, Samhain ("summer's end"), which marked the end of the growing season.

Nature is not a place or a thing. It is a mosaic, a network, a matrix in which is embedded not only the world's biodiversity, but also the day-to-day quality of our lives.

— CHRIS LEAHY, MASSACHUSETTS AUDUBON SOCIETY

TRY THIS

Think through the seasons of the year and what they offer. Plan an activity or celebration for each season. A spring basket of flowers? Fall pumpkin carving or apple picking? A summer bonfire or winter solstice party?

Stay Inspired

Recommendations from the Library of Clare Walker Leslie

Once you begin, everywhere you look there is something more to learn about nature where you are. Joining a nature center, club, or organization can be a great way to learn and to meet people. And although many of us have the Internet at our fingertips these days, there are plenty of field guides to every subject on nature in both the kids' and adult sections of any library or bookstore. As for other books, I have listed below some of the classics from my library that have inspired me and my family to learn about nature. They have stood the test of time. Use this list to branch off and discover your own interests.

Carson, Rachel. *The Sea Around Us*. Oxford University Press, 1951.

——. *The Sense of Wonder*. Harper & Row, 1956.

Dillard, Annie. *Pilgrim at Tinker Creek*. Harper's Magazine Press, 1974.

Grahame, Kenneth. *The Wind in the Willows*. Charles Scribner's Sons, 1908.

Hanh, Thich Nhat. *Love Letter to the Earth*. Parallax Press, 2013.

Haupt, Lyanda Lynn. *Crow Planet: Essential Wisdom from the Urban Wilderness*. Little, Brown and Company, 2009.

Leopold, Aldo. *A Sand County Almanac*. Oxford University Press, 1949.

Louv, Richard. *The Nature Principle: Reconnecting with Life in a Virtual Age*. Algonquin Books, 2011.

Matthews, Anne. *Wild Nights: Nature Returns to the City*. North Point Press, 2001.

Mitchell, John Hanson. *A Field Guide to Your Own Backyard*, 2nd ed. Countryman Press, 2014.

Momaday, N. Scott. *The Way to Rainy Mountain*. University of New Mexico Press, 1969.

Oliver, Mary. *New and Selected Poems*. Beacon Press, 1992.

Pyle, Robert Michael. *The Thunder Tree: Lessons from an Urban Wildland*. Lyons Press, 1993.

Roberts, Elizabeth, and Elias Amidon, eds. *Earth Prayers from Around the World*. Harper San Francisco, 1991.

Safina, Carl. *The View from Lazy Point*. Henry Holt and Co., 2011.

Teale, Edwin Way. *Circle of the Seasons*. Dodd, Mead Co., 1953.

Thoreau, Henry David. *Walden*. Ticknor and Fields, 1854.

Williams, Brian, et al. *Visual Encyclopedia of Science*. Kingfisher Books, 1994.

All you need is your eyes and a moment of time.

Acknowledgments

I WANT TO THANK all who helped this book come into being. These pages are inspired by the years of observation journals I have kept, helping me as a rank beginner to learn more about the world of nature right around where I live. As I don't have a studio per se, the seasonally changing world outdoors has been my constant studio and my journals have always been the place for recording. Keeping these journals, teaching across the country, and exploring outdoors with colleagues as well as family provided the experiences that led to the creation of this book.

I want to thank Deborah Balmuth of Storey Publishing who, as savvy editor and friend, has enabled me to publish five books under her guidance. Hannah Fries and Carolyn Eckert worked hard to get these pages set just right. Working with photographs has been a new experience for me, and the Storey editors were very sensitive to my wondering how drawings and photographs would mesh.

Great thanks goes to my good friend Becci Backman who waded through a year's text preparation with many an hour of subject discussions, tea drinking, and husbands wondering when we would take a break. I want to thank my family for their patience, for giving me ideas, and for observing yet one more book come forth.

It is my hope that this book will give you some of the same curiosity, continual wonder, fascinating learning experiences, and many opportunities to wander outdoors that I have been able to have these last 40 years.

PHOTOGRAPHY CREDITS

© Alan Majchrowicz/Getty Images: 65 (m.)
© alexandrumagurean/iStockphoto.com: 140–141
© Andrea Costa Photography/Getty Images: 104
© Andreas Reh/Getty Images: 66
© Bill Dwight: 23, 26 (all except t.l.)
© Blue Spirit Images/Getty Images: 68–69
© Brandon Flint: 43
© C. Allan Morgan/Getty Images: 65 (t.)
Carolyn Eckert: 15, 32–33, 127 (3rd row l., 4th row l., b.)
© Comstock/Stockbyte/Getty Images: 78
© Daniel A. Leifheit/Getty Images: 53
© Danita Delimont/Getty Images: 83 (3rd row), 113
© danilovi/Getty Images: 8–9
© David Bowman: 71, 91, 102–103,
© David Doubilet/Getty Images: 105
© Dean Casavechia: 80–81
© Don Johnston_IH/Alamy: 95 (t.r., b.l.)
© Dr. Peter Wernicke/Getty Images: 83 (2nd row r.)
© Ed Reschke/Getty Images: 65 (b.), 115 (b.)
© Edwin Rem/NIS/Getty Images: 62 (t.l.)
© Ellen van Bodegom/Getty Images: 62 (b.)
© Eric Frick Photography: 21
© Eric Isselée/lifeonwhite.com/iStockphoto.com: 49
© Eric Lowenbach/Getty Images: 28
© Erika Tirén/MagicAir/Getty Images: 64
© Evan Sheppard: 36 (all), 44–45, 126 (2nd from t.), 127 (2nd row l.), 138
© Felix Meyer/Getty Images: 139
© Fred Hirschmann/Getty Images: 111
© Fuse/Getty Images: 83 (4th row l.)
© Garry DeLong/Alamy: 85
© Graham Monro/gm photographics/Getty Images: 40
© Heather Perry: 3, 12, 26 (t.l.), 126 (t.), 128 (all except m.r.)
© Ian Nixon/Getty Images: (115 m.)
© Images from BarbAnna/Getty Images: 83 (t.)
© James Jordan Photography/Getty Images: 97 (r.)
© Jamie Goldenberg: 6–7, 10, 58, 67, 75, 84, 96, 97 (l.), 100, 101, 114, 126 (3rd row, 4th row l., b. row r.), 127 (t., 2nd row r., 3rd row r., 4th row c. & r.)
© jeffbeckerphotography.com: 131
© Joel Sartore/Getty Images: 61
© 2010 John Grein/Getty Images: 83 (b.l.)
© Josh Andrus: 108–109© Keller + Keller: 1
© Kate Brady/Getty Images: 92
© Leonardo Patrizi/iStockphoto.com: 30
© Mark Fleming Photography: 79, 126 (b.l.)
© Mark Graf/Alamy: 95 (t.l.)
Mars Vilaubi: 17, 63, 73
© Marvin Dembinsky Photo Associates/Alamy (95 b.r.)
© Matthew Carbone: 46–47
© Michael Melford/Getty Images: 112, 134–135
© Michele Doucette: 18–19, 88, 126 (4th row r.), 128 (m.r.)
© Mikel Bilbao/Getty Images: 62 (t.r.)
© Noriyuki Araki/Getty Images: 98
© Peter Baker: 76, 116
© Peter Haigh/Getty Images: 16
© Peter McCabe/Design Pics/Getty Images: 115 (t.)
© Shaunl/Vetta/Getty Images: 50
© Sonja Dahlgren/Getty Images: 74
© South West Images Scotland/Alamy: 136
© Stacey Cramp: 127 (3rd row c.), 132, 144
© Steve & Dave Maslowski/Getty Images: 83 (2nd row l.)
© Thomas Janisch/Getty Images: 83 (4th row r.)
© Thomas Kitchin & Victoria Hurst/Getty Images: 83 (b.r.)
© urbancow/Getty Images: 118

Last Light

May your paths into nature lead you along adventures
full of curiosity, humor, and wonder.

I watch a frog and a frog watches me.

greenfrog
6·10

CLARE WALKER LESLIE is a nationally known wildlife artist, author, and educator. For over 40 years, she has been connecting people of all ages to nature using drawing, writing, and observation of the outdoors. Her 12 books include *The Nature Connection, Nature Journal, Keeping a Nature Journal,* and *Drawn to Nature;* more of her work can be found at clarewalkerleslie.com. She lives with her family in Cambridge, Massachusetts, and Granville, Vermont.

OTHER BOOKS BY CLARE WALKER LESLIE

SILVER NAUTILUS AWARD WINNER

"Fascinating, inspirational, and beautifully illustrated, *The Curious Nature Guide* ~~is the perfect b~~ook for anyone looking ~~to renew their~~ connection with the natural world."

—RICHARD LOUV, author of *Last Child in the Woods* and *The Nature Principle*

ISBN 978-1-61212-509-1

EAN

9 781612 125091

51495

NATURE $14.95 US

Storey
www.storey.com